WESTCHESTER PUBLIC LIBRARY

3 1310 00304 8531

S0-BXY-403

FACTS AND FICTION ABOUT DRUGS™

METHAMPHETAMINES

ALEXIS BURLING

rosen publishing's
rosen
central®

New York

TEEN
613.84
BUR

Published in 2020 by The Rosen Publishing Group, Inc.
29 East 21st Street, New York, NY 10010

Copyright © 2020 by The Rosen Publishing Group, Inc.

First Edition

All rights reserved. No part of this book may be reproduced in any form without permission in writing from the publisher, except by a reviewer.

Library of Congress Cataloging-in-Publication Data

Names: Burling, Alexis, author.
Title: Methamphetamines / Alexis Burling.
Description: New York : Rosen Publishing, 2020 | Series: Facts and fiction about drugs | Includes bibliographical references and index. | Audience: Grades 5–8.
Identifiers: LCCN 2019010064 | ISBN 9781725347588 (library bound) | ISBN 9781725347571 (pbk.)
Subjects: LCSH: Methamphetamine abuse—Juvenile literature. | Ice (Drug)—Juvenile literature. | Drug abuse—Juvenile literature.
Classification: LCC RC568.A45 B85 2020 | DDC 362.29/95—dc23
LC record available at https://lccn.loc.gov/2019010064

Some of the images in this book illustrate individuals who are models. The depictions do not imply actual situations or events.

Manufactured in the United States of America

CONTENTS

INTRODUCTION

In 1999, when Nic Sheff was seventeen years old, he had one of his first experiences with love. But it wasn't with a person. He had become infatuated with one of the deadliest illegal drugs: methamphetamine, commonly referred to as meth.

Sheff's path to meth addiction started early. He first experimented with marijuana when he was twelve. When smoking pot no longer offered enough of a high, he looked for harder drugs. He tried mushrooms, prescription pills like OxyContin, and cocaine. But it wasn't until he used meth that Sheff felt he had finally found "the one."

"As soon as that drug hit me, I felt a rush of elation—not just from the drug, but from feeling like this was what I'd been looking for my whole life. It was better than those first hits of pot, better than *everything*," Sheff wrote in *High*, the book he coauthored with his father, David. "I felt like a real-life superhero. Just like that I was addicted."

For Sheff, using meth didn't begin as an everyday occurrence. But quickly, it became a persistent habit—and a dangerous one. He broke into houses to steal money to pay for the drug. His parents kicked him out of the house. His body fell apart.

Sheff nearly died from his meth addiction. But after more than ten years of trying—and failing—to get clean, he kicked the habit for good. He is the author of two memoirs, *Tweak: Growing Up on Methamphetamines* and *We All Fall Down: Living with Addiction*. The story of his drug addiction was made into the 2018 award-winning movie *Beautiful Boy*.

Since the publication of his first book, *Tweak,* in 2008, author Nic Sheff has spoken to audiences nationwide about his former meth addiction and long struggle to get clean.

But not all meth users successfully beat their habit. In fact, meth is one of the most destructive drugs there is. According to the Centers for Disease Control and Prevention (CDC), in 2017, meth was a factor in more than ten thousand overdose deaths in the United States.

Meth abuse is a worldwide issue. But drug addiction isn't a character flaw; it's a crippling and hard to cure disease. Knowing what meth is, how it affects the mind and body, and how to treat an addiction is the best first step toward dealing with this epidemic.

CHAPTER ONE

What Is Meth?

As of 2019, thirty-six-year-old Nic Sheff is an accomplished author and a television writer. He's also happily married. But because of his drug habit, his successful career and marriage almost didn't happen.

Addiction to meth is a serious problem. It affects all parts of society, regardless of age, race, gender, or income level. According to the Substance Abuse and Mental Health Services Administration (SAMHSA), in 2017, around 774,000 people aged twelve or older were current users of meth. So what exactly is meth? And why is it so easy to get hooked on it?

Meth is a type of drug called a stimulant, a drug that speeds up the brain. It allows users to feel awake for long periods of time. It also improves concentration. After taking the drug, meth users usually need less sleep to get through the day. They can do daily tasks like cleaning the house or homework without losing energy.

Methamphetamines come in many forms, including pills, powder, and tiny rocklike crystals called crystal meth. The drug can be snorted, injected, swallowed, or smoked.

Similar to other drugs, meth comes in many forms: pills, powder, or tiny rocklike crystals called ice. It also has many names. Speed, glass, tweak, chalk, Tina, Chrissy, Christmas tree, crank, and gak are just some of the common slang terms for the drug.

The purest form is the crystalized version, nicknamed crystal meth. The drug looks like shards of glass or tiny rocks. People start out by using crystal meth or other forms of meth for fun at dance clubs or parties. The more often they do it, the harder it is to stop.

A BRIEF HISTORY OF METHAMPHETAMINES

Today meth is mostly a drug people do for fun. But it wasn't always the case. In fact, meth was invented by a Japanese scientist. Nagai Nagayoshi discovered the chemical in 1893. He created it as a man-made substitute for ephedrine, an extract from a plant used in Chinese medicine for thousands of years. Then in 1919, another Japanese chemist named Akira Ogata made the drug easier to use. He created the world's first crystalized meth.

Meth was outlawed in the United States in 1970. But before then, it was used to treat asthma and a sleep disorder called narcolepsy. People also took the drug to lose weight. During World War II, soldiers even used it to stay awake during battle.

How Meth Is Made

Many drugs, such as cocaine or marijuana, come from plants. But meth is fully synthetic. That means it is made from a chemical, or man-made, source. Making meth is not only a complicated process, it's also potentially deadly.

Meth is manufactured in one of two ways. One method takes place in homes or illegal laboratories. People referred to as cookers mix stimulants called amphetamines with other household chemicals. Sometimes, as with crystal meth, the drug is pure and more potent. Other times, cookers mix in chemical ingredients found in nail polish remover, batteries, drain cleaner, and cold medicine. Additions like antifreeze or paint thinner can cause a meth user to behave in erratic ways.

The other way to make meth happens much more quickly. Sometimes when users become desperate to find more of the drug,

An investigator for the Oklahoma County Sherrif's Department demonstates how dangerous it is to cook meth by wearing a mask, gloves, and a hazardous materials suit.

they make it themselves. They combine various chemicals in a plastic bottle. Then they shake it until crystals form. But following this method, or even making the drug in a lab, can be very unsafe.

Cooking meth means working with potentially flammable chemicals. If cookers combine these chemicals in an incorrect way, an explosion could occur. Many cookers have been seriously injured. Others have died in meth lab fires. Sometimes even uninhabited meth labs can be dangerous. According to the United States Department of Agriculture (USDA), "abandoned meth labs are basically time bombs, waiting for the single spark that can ignite the contents of the lab."

HOW TO SPOT A METH LAB

Meth labs are dangerous and should be avoided at all costs. There are a few common signs to tell if you have come upon a meth lab. The USDA advises people to look out for the following:

- Run-down shacks or houses with blacked-out windows
- Lots of trash around the house, including large amounts of empty antifreeze containers, nail polish remover, fuel cans, or empty battery packages
- A strong, unpleasant odor that sometimes smells like urine
- Glass pots or frying pans with powdery residue
- Coffee filters containing a white, sticky substance

People who stumble upon a working or abandoned meth lab should be extremely careful. They should never touch anything or open any containers. Handling meth waste residue can burn the skin and eyes. Breathing in the gas can also be lethal.

There's also another problem: toxic waste. Meth labs harm the environment. Some cookers dump hazardous materials into rivers or bury them in the ground. Much of this waste can easily catch fire or explode. According to the USDA, 1 pound (0.5 kg) of meth produces 6 pounds (2.7 kg) of toxic waste. It contaminates septic systems. It leaks into the drinking water. It also kills plants and animals.

How Meth Is Used

Meth is one of the riskiest illegal drugs to make. But in many cases, it is also one of the least expensive to buy. Because it costs as little as $5 a hit, it is popular with young adults and people of all economic backgrounds. It can be swallowed, snorted, injected with a needle, or smoked.

Crank is a less-pure form of crystal meth. It's often cheaper because it is cut with other man-made substances. It is usually snorted, smoked, or injected. Users can consume crank by eating it, but this method does not produce as strong of a high.

Many meth users report being attracted to the drug because of its immediate short-term effects. Doing meth boosts energy levels. It also helps users feel more confident.

But there's a downside. A meth high always triggers a crash, a period of deep depression and anxiety. Users do increasingly higher doses to pick themselves up after a crash. They then need more of the drug to maintain the same level of high. Some meth abusers become so desperate that they take the drug every few hours. They give up food and sleep so the drug's effects are stronger.

Buying, selling, or cooking meth is illegal in the United States. Addicts can go to jail if they're caught.

Whether it is smoked, snorted, or injected, meth is one of the most addictive drugs available. Meth is also very unhealthy. It temporarily alters the way a person feels, acts, and thinks. It also permanently destroys parts of the brain and body.

CHAPTER TWO

Meth and the Brain

When Corey Ary was growing up in the small town of Belle Plaine, Iowa, during the 1990s, he seemed to have everything. He had a bunch of close friends and a good family. But suddenly, everything changed.

When Ary was fourteen, he started hanging out with a different crowd. These friends smoked pot and drank alcohol. He stole his dad's truck and tried crack cocaine. Then he made a leap that would change the course of his life forever. He smoked meth for the first time. Then he immediately wanted more.

"When you smoke meth, it's like everything in the world is interesting," Ary said in a 2018 interview with KWWL News in Iowa. "I would go until I fell out. I would stay up for days and days, and then sleep for a couple hours, or whenever I fell out, I would keep going."

Before long, Ary was addicted. He became agitated, started fighting with his parents, and rarely went to school. Then he started selling the drug for easier access. He was arrested and was sent to jail more than a dozen times.

"I would be gone for literally like six months at a time and never have to go back home. I would live on the road," Ary said. "My mom would literally be thankful whenever she got that call I was in jail that I was actually safe."

For fourteen years, Ary chased after the feeling of his first meth high. He was hospitalized three times. By February 2018, his body had deteriorated. So had his brain. According to Ary, he hit rock bottom. He didn't know who he was, what day it was, or how to do basic things like tie his shoes. He had lost touch with reality.

Meth addiction can have many negative consequences. Abusers may become violent, steal, or commit other crimes when under the influence of the drug. They may even be arrested for their crimes.

"I wanted to be dead. I was trying to pretty much kill myself by using drugs," Ary told KWWL. "I almost succeeded making myself brain dead."

Meth started out as a "fun" substance Ary tried before he even had his driver's license. It soon changed into a near-lethal addiction that almost ruined his mind. Thankfully, in May 2018 Ary got sober. But his body is still recovering after too many years of abuse. Out of all the drugs available, meth has some of the most gruesome and long-lasting effects on the brain.

Short-Term Effects

In order to get high from meth, smoking or injecting the drug is the quickest method for delivery. The rush happens right away. It delivers a brief, but intense, sensation throughout the head and body. Snorting or taking the drug orally produces a longer-lasting high. Sometimes the feeling can last as long as ten hours.

After meth is ingested, it travels from the nose, throat, or lungs and makes its way to the brain. There, it causes nerve cells to release a neurotransmitter called dopamine, which triggers pleasure signals. Under normal circumstances, such as eating delicious food or doing fun activities like listening to music or jumping on a trampoline, the brain releases small amounts of dopamine. This substance allows a person to feel happy. But meth causes the brain to produce between ten and twenty times the normal amount of dopamine. When this flood is released, a person experiences a high. It feels like floating on a cloud.

In the short term, the effects are deceptively positive. Focusing on tasks becomes easier. Tiredness vanishes. Many meth users report feeling confident, sharp-witted, and more capable when doing mentally demanding tasks such as studying for a test or writing a paper.

But these effects are short-lived. Even after the first hit, meth can cause anxiety and nervousness. Some users become hypersensitive to bright light, loud sounds, or touch. While these effects might sound uncomfortable, the long-term effects are even worse. After all, the more meth a person does, the more harm it does to the brain.

Long-Term Effects

Drug addiction happens because users take a substance repeatedly over short periods of time. They can't seem to stop. In Corey Ary's case, he quickly developed a tolerance for meth. Therefore, he needed to do the drug more often— and to do more of it each time—in order to regain the experience of his original high and avoid a crash.

What's more, the more meth people do, the less pleasure they're able to feel doing the activities that used to make them happy. For this reason, people who use meth can easily become depressed. Chronic

Meth can cause the brain to act like it's received a prolonged jolt of electricity. Many meth users report feeling wide awake, clearheaded, and hyperfocused for long periods of time.

THIS IS YOUR BRAIN ON METH

Meth affects a user's cognitive abilities and motor skills. But it also has long-lasting effects on the way the brain looks and functions. Under normal circumstances, someone who doesn't use drugs has a lot of nonneural brain cells called microglia. They protect the brain from infectious agents. Microglial cells also get rid of the brain's damaged neurons.

In a meth user's brain, the microglial cells behave differently. According to a study published in the *Journal of Neuroscience* in 2008, people who use meth have more than twice the amount of microglia in their brains than people with no history of doing the drug. This is dangerous for many reasons. If there are too many microglial cells, they can start attacking healthy neurons instead. The study also found that meth's long-term effects on the brain can last for at least fourteen months or longer. Depending on the length of abuse of the drug, some meth addicts' brains never heal.

meth abusers may not be able to feel any pleasure at all other than that provided by the drug. This situation makes quitting seem impossible.

Aside from altering the way the brain works, the most harmful effect of chronic drug use is addiction. It's a brain disease that occurs when people use a drug all the time, despite negative consequences. They become dependent on the drug in order to function normally.

As a direct result of their addiction, chronic abusers exhibit a wide range of symptoms. They can experience near-constant anxiety, confusion, and have a hard time focusing on simple tasks. Memory loss is possible. Insomnia, paranoia, and severe moodiness are common. Many meth users are aggressive or violent. They might also become psychotic.

One of the scariest side effects of using meth is an increased possibility of delusions. This means addicts see things or hear sounds that aren't there. For example, many meth addicts hear voices or complain that insects are crawling under their skin.

These types of psychotic symptoms can last for months or even years after a person has stopped using meth. In some particularly extreme cases, loud noises or a stressful situation can trigger delusions even after an addict has stopped using.

Dr. Doug Melzer is a physician who works in the emergency room (ER) at St. Patrick Hospital in Missoula, Montana. He treats patients for a wide variety of ailments, including pneumonia, heart attacks, or injuries from car accidents. He also treats meth addicts who come to the emergency room during a binge.

According to Dr. Melzer, when these meth addicts stumble into the ER, they are usually

Meth can cause extreme anxiety if used for a long period of time. Many addicts have ended up in the emergency room because they have tried to rip the hair out of their heads or skin.

hallucinating—and extremely freaked out. Often, they become violent. In one particularly frightening instance, a patient ripped a security camera out of a hospital room ceiling. Another punched a giant hole in the wall. Sometimes meth user patients can be so wild that it takes six or seven medics to strap them to a hospital bed and inject them with a tranquilizer to calm them down.

"A lot of times we'll even take the bed out of [the room] and just leave the mattress on the floor," Dr. Melzer told a reporter for Meth Effect, an online publication from the University of Montana School of Journalism. "[Addicts] can literally pick up these hundred-pound beds and throw them against the wall."

In places like hospital emergency rooms, it's easy to witness some of the disastrous effects meth can have on a person's brain. But Dr. Melzer warns that brain damage is only half of the story. Unfortunately, the drug's effects on the body are just as terrible.

CHAPTER THREE

Meth and the Body

Greg and Mary Haydal had what many people might call an enviable life. After years of marriage, they were still in love. They owned a beautiful ranch in Miles City, Montana. They had two daughters, Cassie and Nicole. They raised horses, dogs, and cats. The girls' grandparents lived nearby.

Greg and Mary's situation seemed perfect. But little did they know that their lives were about to take a dark turn. Their eldest daughter, Cassie, had everything going for her. She was a senior in high school with excellent grades. She coached basketball and wrote articles about sports for the local newspaper. Montana State University had accepted her and she planned to study journalism there.

But the Haydals had also noticed a change in their daughter. Over the course of her senior year, Cassie had lost a lot of weight. She barely slept and had developed dark circles under her eyes. Sometimes she seemed anxious. They took her to a

Since losing her daughter to a meth addiction, Mary Haydal, shown here, has spoken to people all over the country about the dangers of the drug.

doctor to treat a bad cough that wouldn't go away. Greg and Mary were worried. But they assumed that Cassie was just being a typical teenager.

Then the unthinkable happened. One day after school, Cassie came home from coaching her sister's basketball team. As soon as she entered the kitchen, she collapsed. Mary tried to wake her up while a neighbor called an ambulance. When they got to the hospital and the doctors ran some tests, they told Mary her daughter had suffered a heart attack. She was in a coma and had irreversible brain damage. Cassie's heart attack and eventual death happened because of a terrible secret.

Unbeknownst to her parents, she had been addicted to meth for more than a year.

"We thought we lost Cassie because we were bad parents," Mary Haydal wrote in a November 2018 blog post for Get Smart About Drugs (www.getsmartaboutdrugs.gov), a Drug Enforcement Administration website for parents and educators. "Where were we as methamphetamine ravaged our child's mind, body and life? How could we stare it in the face every day and not see it?"

Haydal's reaction is not uncommon for loved ones of drug users. Sometimes it can be difficult to spot an addiction until it's too late. It's important to know the signs of meth abuse, including how it can cause short- and long-term harm to the body.

Short-Term Effects

According to experts, one of the easiest ways to spot a meth user is by looking at his or her eyes. Paying attention to body language is important, too. Meth causes the pupils to dilate, or grow larger. It also disrupts natural sleep patterns and appetite. Most meth addicts

There are a range of signs that show someone is addicted to meth, including weight loss, jittery behavior, and missing teeth.

avoid eating and can't sleep for more than a few hours at a time. They lose weight and develop dark circles under their eyes.

Doing meth increases respiration. Chronic users take short but rapid breaths, like they can't get enough air into their lungs. The drug can also cause a fast or irregular heartbeat and increase blood pressure. Many people who abuse meth complain of hyperthermia, or elevated body temperature. It's not unusual to see an addict walking around in the cold weather wearing a tank top or thin pants.

For people who use needles, there's also a very visual side effect. Similar to heroin abusers, addicts who inject meth into their veins get red, irritated marks on their arms, between their

THE RISK OF DISEASE

Like any drug user who uses needles, meth injectors are at greater risk for infectious diseases like HIV/AIDS or hepatitis C. These illnesses are transmitted through contact with blood or other bodily fluids. Meth use can also alter judgment and a person's ability to make smart decisions. Sometimes people who use meth participate in risky behavior, such as unprotected sex. This risky behavior can increase the chance of infection.

If a meth user already has a disease, fighting the illness becomes that much harder. The body doesn't have enough strength. For example, studies show that HIV causes greater damage to nerve cells in people who have HIV and do meth than it does in people who have the disease and don't use the drug.

toes, or wherever they insert the drug. They are called track marks. If not cared for properly, these wounds can get infected.

Long-Term Effects

Similar to the way meth degrades the brain, the longer a meth addict uses, the more damage meth does to the body. Perhaps the grossest side effect of long-term meth use is called meth mouth. It happens because the drug reduces the amount of protective saliva around the teeth. Meth also eats away at tooth enamel. Consequently, mouth ulcers are common.

To make matters worse, many meth addicts have poor hygiene habits. They also maintain a sugary diet, a common cause of tooth decay and gum disease. They can suffer from bruxism, or excessive teeth grinding, due to constant twitching and feeling jittery. As a result of this unhealthy combination, teeth can become cracked or rotten, turn brown, and fall out. Addicts who have lost some or all of their teeth have to "gum" their food when eating.

Inmate Jeffrey Lotshaw shows his toothless mouth at the Maryville Treatment Center in Maryville, Missouri. He lost all of his teeth as a result of heavy methamphetamine use.

In addition to oral hygiene issues, meth affects the skin and nose. Addicts suffering from visual hallucinations often obsessively scratch their skin, causing deep scars. Acne is common, as are wrinkles. The skin loses some of its stretchiness and takes on a leatherlike appearance. People who snort meth are at risk of losing their septum, the piece of the nose that separates the nostrils.

Aside from the visual effects, meth destroys the body from the inside out. Anyone who tries the drug even once has an increased risk of stroke. Chronic use causes severe damage to the blood vessels. The heart muscle can get inflamed and aortic ruptures are possible. The liver and kidneys can stop working properly. A violent, ongoing cough can cause lung collapse. Any of these conditions can be fatal.

Overdosing on Meth

Despite all the terrifying side effects, people still try meth—and choose to continue doing it. Most users want to use the drug constantly without going overboard. But sometimes an overdose—doing too much—is unintentional.

An overdose occurs when a person snorts, injects, or inhales too much of a drug and has a toxic reaction. Overdosing can cause a heart attack, stroke, seizures, kidney failure, and brain bleeds. It can also lead to death.

Over the last decade, meth use has increased in the United States. Overdoses have become more common. In fact, according to a 2019 article by Dan Vergano in BuzzFeed, more than seventy thousand people a year die of drug overdoses in the United States. That's more deaths than fatalities caused by car crashes, guns, or AIDS-related deaths during the 1990s.

Given the growing crisis, medical experts insist it's important to know the warning signs of an overdose in order to spot when it might occur. The first clue is an elevated heart rate. Body shakes, an irregular heartbeat, and excessively high body temperature are also possible. People in the midst of an overdose are often covered in sweat.

Meth overdoses can happen to a person of any age, race, gender, or color. People who mix meth with other dangerous drugs, such as heroin, prescription drugs, or even alcohol, increase their risk of an overdose. It's also possible to overdose on meth the very first time one tries it. Witnessing a drug overdose is scary. Experiencing one can sometimes be fatal. But there are other important consequences of meth addiction. Whether it's the emotional fallout that comes with doing the drug or dealing with withdrawal, meth addiction is nearly impossible to endure.

The Consequences of Addiction

Christine Suhan once spent an entire day picking dirt out of the carpet. But she wasn't trying to make sure it was clean. She was looking for crystal meth. Two weeks later, she was back on the floor again. But this time, it was because she couldn't feel her arms and legs. She couldn't walk or stand. Suhan was in the middle of an overdose.

Suhan almost died. But the terrifying experience didn't faze her. Once she was out of the hospital, Suhan picked up where she left off. Two weeks later, she overdosed again. As soon as she recovered from her second overdose, she started injecting meth instead of just smoking and snorting it.

"If you had told me in high school that carpet-picking, needles, overdoses, and psychotic breaks from reality would have been part of my life story, I would have laughed in your face," Suhan told *Marie Claire* in 2015. "I was a good girl; I was smart and made good grades. I was an all-star athlete who came from a great family. I had no reason to use drugs."

Once Suhan started doing meth, the drug quickly took over her life. She didn't know how to stop. She lost friends. She got fired from multiple jobs. Most of her family stopped speaking to her. She was thrown in jail and lost her driver's license. Still, Suhan didn't want to give up the one thing that supposedly made her happy.

"I didn't plan for this to be my life," Suhan said. "But the disease of addiction does not discriminate. Addiction didn't care

Meth addiction is difficult for everyone involved. Many addicts feel like a disappointment to their parents, while parents are concerned that their children won't survive.

that I was smart or that I came from a loving family. Addiction didn't care what kind of life I had planned."

Personal and Social Fallout

Christine Suhan's story is very sad. But as seen with Nic Sheff, Corey Ary, and Cassie Haydal, Suhan's situation is far too common. For many drug users, an overdose isn't a wakeup call. It's just a temporary obstacle to getting high. For family members and friends of people addicted to meth or other drugs, dealing with this type of life-threatening behavior can be frustrating. It can also be hard to figure out the difference between a one-time experiment with drugs and a full-blown addiction.

The progression from drug user to drug addict starts slowly. First, small changes are noticeable. Normal behavioral patterns shift. Meth users might eat less or seem distracted more often. They might not seem interested in doing activities that used to bring them joy. Younger meth users might notice that their grades drop, either from lack of concentration or from not attending classes.

Changes in friend groups or a romantic partner are also common. Sometimes meth users stop talking to loved ones who act judgmental, even if those friends and family members are only trying to help. As the addiction becomes more serious, meth users might become more aggressive. Because they need the drug and the high it gives them, they'll often stop at nothing to get their hands on another hit. This need can lead to stealing or other crimes. Some meth addicts resort to selling drugs or living on the street. Others have unprotected sex with strangers or their dealers in order to get the drug.

DOS AND DON'TS

Do pay attention to the warning signs of meth addiction. If they are happening, chances are there's a problem.
Don't ignore the problem. It won't go away on its own.

Do try to find someone you trust who can help. This person can be a parent or guardian, teacher, doctor, guidance counselor, or other authority figure.
Don't stay quiet about the situation. That's not doing anyone any good—especially the addict. But don't blab about it all over school. Spreading gossip can have unintended consequences.

Do call the police if the addict becomes threatening or violent and you think you, the addict, or anyone else involved could be in danger.
Don't rely solely on the police. While the police can help with law enforcement, sometimes the situation is better handled by a medical professional.

Do educate yourself on the facts of drug abuse and meth in particular. Knowledge is power. It can also save lives.
Don't listen to or spread rumors about meth and its effects.

For friends and family members, it can be tricky to know how to help. Some stage a carefully planned meeting called an intervention, either with the help of professional drug counselors or on their own. In the meeting, they confront their loved ones about the addiction and try to get them to stop. The addict may feel attacked and accuse others of tricking him.

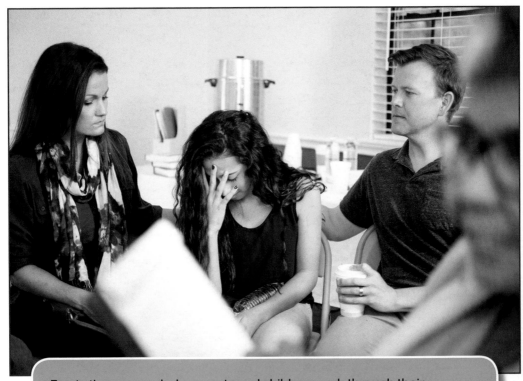

Famiy therapy can help parents and children work through their issues in a safe space. This can be challenging for all involved but is an important step in helping the addict recover.

But even addicts who want to quit face an uphill battle. Once a person starts using meth on a regular basis, getting off the drug becomes that much harder. Though it's a necessary struggle to go through in order to get clean, the withdrawal process is awful for everyone involved.

The Withdrawal Spiral

With cases of drug addiction, there's no middle ground. The only way out is to stop doing the drug, either gradually or all at once. The process takes a long time. Relapses, or cycles of using

TOUGH LOVE PROS AND CONS

Drug addicts can do great harm to their family and friends. Sometimes they lie or ask for large amounts of money. Other times they steal valuables or damage property. For some people, this repeated behavior can get to be too much. Instead of writing one more check, they just stop trying to help. This approach is called tough love. It's when loved ones treat addicts harshly—not to be mean, but to help them heal or inspire them to seek treatment.

Some experts consider tough love to be a valuable tool when dealing with drug addiction, especially as a last resort if all other methods have failed. David Sheff disagrees. "Addiction is a disease like anything else ... At the first signs of serious illness, we want to intervene," he said in a 2018 interview on the National Public Radio (NPR) program *Fresh Air*. "If you love someone who's an addict and their use is life-threatening, you don't wait until they hit bottom because that can mean that they're going to die. You have to do everything you can to get them in treatment."

again, happen more often than not. But in order to get better, an addict must stop doing the drug completely.

Withdrawal symptoms range in intensity, depending on the level of addiction. Some physical symptoms include muscle aches, nerve pain, and chills. Involuntary shaking in the arms, legs, hands, and feet is also usual.

Mentally, withdrawal is brutal, too. People trying to wean themselves off meth usually become agitated, restless, or overly emotional. They can fly into a rage or become violent. The rate of success is low. Many drug addicts who try to get sober report thinking about suicide. Coming off a drug, especially one as harmful as meth, is agonizing. If at all possible, it shouldn't be done unsupervised.

But though recovery is excruciating, it is not impossible. The first step is asking friends or family members for help. More often than not, professional or medical assistance is suggested, if not required. Whether it's outpatient therapy or inpatient rehab, twenty-four-hour hotlines or an outdoor wellness program, seeking help is the most important step drug users can take in getting their life back on track.

Getting Help

Meth use has risen across the world. According to SAMHSA's 2017 National Survey on Drug Use and Health, about 16,000 adolescents in the United States, aged twelve to seventeen, were current meth users. Approximately 151,000 young adults in the United States, aged eighteen to twenty-five, used the drug in the past month. Around 607,000 adults in the United States, aged twenty-six or older, did meth regularly.

"Usage of methamphetamine nationally is at an all-time high," says Erik Smith, assistant special agent in charge of the Drug Enforcement Administration's Kansas City office told NPR in 2018. "It is back with a vengeance."

Not all meth addicts seek help for their addiction, however. According to SAMHSA's survey, nearly 21 million people in the United States, aged twelve or older, needed substance abuse treatment in 2017. However, only 4 million received any help.

For many addicts or family members of addicts, knowing what to do or where to go to fix the problem can be a daunting process. But there are trained professionals who can help. Whether it's through a national hotline, regular appointments with a licensed drug counselor, or inpatient drug rehabilitation, finding the right method of care is key to breaking the habit and getting healthy again.

Outpatient Therapy

One of the most convenient options for drug addiction treatment is outpatient therapy. If the situation isn't that serious, there are different types of outpatient treatments that teach people with drug addictions how to change their behavior surrounding drug use. Certified drug counseling a couple times a week is a

In addition to treatment at an inpatient or outpatient facility, some meth users try alternative therapies, such as yoga and meditation, to calm their thoughts and ease withdrawal symptoms.

great first step. If the addict is younger, family counseling is also an option. But kids and teens should always be treated independently as well. Sometimes a family member is part of the problem.

In addition to traditional treatments, there are alternative methods that help the body heal physically. Meditation is a calming activity that is helpful for some addicts. They meditate by sitting quietly with their eyes closed and letting their mind go blank. Acupuncture is another method. This practice involves a trained practitioner who sticks tiny needles into parts of the body to take away pressure or pain. Each of these practices is guided by a professional and helps addicts focus more on being healthy rather than fixating on their drug cravings.

Inpatient Rehab

No one treatment is right for everyone. For more serious cases, in-patient rehab centers are the way to go. Addicts stay in a hospital or other facility for a period of time. They take drug education classes and participate in group therapy sessions. Medical professionals are there to help them withdraw from the drug. Some programs last for six weeks. Others can go on for a year or more.

Some rehab centers are free or are either completely or partially covered by health insurance programs. But many cost money. For example, in 2018, outpatient detox programs ranged from $1,000 to $1,500 in total on average. Inpatient rehab centers may cost about $6,000 for a thirty-day program. Well-known centers can cost up to $20,000 for the same length of time. For longer programs, the cost could range anywhere from $12,000 to $60,000. This high price tag might be too expensive for some families, especially if their health insurance doesn't offer drug treatment coverage.

Two other options are wilderness therapy programs and checking into a halfway house. Wilderness therapy is a type of detox program that is run by trained mental health and substance abuse counselors. They take addicts out of their comfort zones and send them on month-long or multimonth excursions in the woods in order to help them develop more positive coping strategies and kick their drug habit in the process. Halfway houses help addicts recover after treatment. They assist them in finding a job, going back to school, and reconnecting with loved ones. In many ways, counselors at halfway houses help recovering addicts reenter society.

Maintaining a Support System

Recovering from drug abuse is one of the hardest things to do. Relapses, or doing drugs again, are common. They are caused by triggers, such as environment or relationship stresses, money worries, or physical cravings. They can also happen if a former addict reconnects with

Although it might not always seem possible, people can kick a meth habit. Love and support from family and friends is a great place to start.

RELIABLE RESOURCES

If you or someone you know is struggling with a drug problem, it can be difficult to find reliable resources that provide fact-based information about what meth is and how to get help. Aside from talking to a teacher, librarian, or other trustworthy authority figure, here are some places to start:

- **SAMHSA's National Helpline**: 1-800-662-HELP (4357). A confidential, free, twenty-four-hour-a-day, 365-day-a-year, information service, in English and Spanish.
- **National Suicide Prevention Lifeline**: 1-800-273-TALK (8255). A hotline for people who are having suicidal thoughts or know someone who is suicidal, with an online chat option.
- **National Institute on Drug Abuse's Kid-Friendly Web Portal**: https://www.drugabuse.gov/children-and-teens. A section of NIDA's website devoted specifically to getting kids helpful information on drugs and how to get help.
- **Scholastic Heads Up**: http://headsup.scholastic.com. A packed web portal full of real news about drugs and your body, for students.

old drug-using friends. According to NIDA, between 40 and 60 percent of recovering addicts fall into this trap. Some are in and out of rehab centers many times.

Meth addiction can happen to anyone. Quitting is incredibly challenging. But with the proper help—and plenty of love and support—overcoming a drug habit for good is possible. Though it might not seem that way at times, a healthy life is never too far out of reach.

AMPHETAMINES Drugs that cause the nervous system to speed up and become more active so that a person feels more energy and excitement.

ANTIFREEZE A liquid people put in their car to cool off the engine.

COGNITIVE Involving conscious mental activities, such as thinking, learning, and remembering.

COMA A physical state in which a person is unable to wake up for a long period of time.

CONTAMINATE To make something dirty by adding something harmful to it.

CRYSTAL METH An illegal and toxic drug in the form of crystals that causes a user to feel more energetic and alert when one smokes it.

DETOX To stop using a drug and allow the body to get rid of its toxic effects.

DOPAMINE A neurotransmitter that sends pleasure signals to the brain.

ELATION An emotional state of great happiness or wonder.

GRUESOME Extremely gross, gory, or unpleasant.

HALLUCINATIONS Images, sounds, or smells that seem real but don't actually exist, usually caused by mental illness or the effect of a drug.

INTERVENTION When a group of family members and/or friends gets together and confronts an addict about his or her drug habit.

OVERDOSE An amount of a drug that is too much to take and is potentially life-threatening.

POTENT Having great power, strength, or effect.

STIMULANT A type of drug that makes users feel more active and energized.

TOLERANCE The body's ability to adjust to a drug so that its effects are felt less strongly.

Canadian Centre on Substance Abuse and Addiction
75 Albert Street, Suite 500
Ottawa, ON K1P 5E7
Canada
(833) 235-4048
Website: http://www.ccdus.ca
Facebook: @CCSA.CCDUS
Twitter: @CCSACanada
This organization works to address issues related to substance use
and addiction that affect the health and safety of Canadians. It
provides education, links to resources, and prevention strategies.

D.A.R.E. America
PO Box 512090
Los Angeles, CA 90051-0090
(800) 223-DARE or (310) 215-0575
Website: https://www.dare.org
Facebook: @DAREINTERNATIONAL
D.A.R.E. (Drug Abuse Resistance Education) aims to educate kids
and young adults about the dangers of drug use and addiction.
The program is offered in 75 percent of schools in the United
States and in more than fifty-two countries around the world.

Drug Free America Foundation, Inc.
5999 Central Avenue, Suite 301
Saint Petersburg, FL 33710
(727) 828-0211

Website: https://dfaf.org
Facebook: @DrugFreeAmericaFndn
Instagram: @drugfreeamericafoundation
Twitter: @DrugFreeAmerica
The mission of this drug prevention and policy organization is to
develop and promote national and international policies and laws
that will help stop illegal drug use and drug addiction. The
group's efforts include Students Taking Action Not Drugs
(STAND), a division dedicated to distributing information on
drugs and addiction to students nationwide.

Drug Free Kids Canada
Corus Quay
25 Dockside Drive
Toronto, ON M5A 0B5
Canada
(416) 479-6972
Website: https://www.drugfreekidscanada.org
Facebook: @DrugFreeKidsCanada
Twitter: @DrugFreeKidsCda
This nonprofit organization is dedicated to educating adults and kids
about the dangers of drug abuse and addiction.

Just Think Twice
Drug Enforcement Administration Headquarters
Community Outreach Support and Prevention Section
8701 Morrisette Drive
Springfield, VA, 22152
(833) 235-4048
Website: https://www.justthinktwice.gov
Facebook: @deaedfoundation

Twitter: @DEAHQ
Created by the Drug Enforcement Administration (DEA) specifically for young people, this site provides information about drugs and drug addiction.

National Council on Alcoholism and Drug Dependence (NCADD)
217 Broadway, Suite 712
New York, NY 10007
(212) 269-7797
Website: https://www.ncadd.org
Facebook: @facingaddiction
Twitter: @NCADDNational
This organization provides public education about drug abuse and alcoholism. Its website posts treatment resources and uplifting stories of people going through the recovery process.

National Institute on Drug Abuse for Teens (NIDA)
National Institutes of Health
9000 Rockville Pike
Bethesda, MD 20892
(301) 496-4000
Website: https://teens.drugabuse.gov
Facebook: @NIDANIH
Twitter: @NIDAnews
This organization is part of the National Institute on Drug Abuse (NIDA), National Institutes of Health (NIH), and the US Department of Health and Human Services. Its teen-friendly website contains useful information about drugs, their effects, addiction, and how to get help.

Ambrose, Marylou, and Veronica Deisler. *Investigate Methamphetamine.* Berkeley Heights, NJ: Enslow Publishers, 2015.

Bryan, Bethany. *Methamphetamine and Stimulant Abuse.* New York, NY: Rosen Publishing, 2019.

Edwards, Sue Bradford. *Meth.* Minneapolis, MN: Abdo Publishing, 2019.

Hillstrom, Kevin. *Methamphetamine.* Farmington Hills, MI: Lucent Books, 2015.

Kenney, Karen. *The Hidden Story of Drugs* (Undercover Story). New York, NY: Rosen Publishing, 2014.

Landau, Jennifer. *Teens Talk About Drugs and Alcohol* (Teen Voices: Real Teens Discuss Real Problems). New York, NY: Rosen Publishing, 2017.

McKenzie, Precious. *Helping a Friend with a Drug Problem* (How Can I Help? Friends Helping Friends). New York, NY: Rosen Publishing, 2017.

Parker, Chance. *A Kid's Guide to Drugs and Alcohol.* Vestal, NY: Village Earth Press, 2016.

Perritano, John. *Stimulants: Meth, Cocaine, and Amphetamines.* Broomall, PA: Mason Crest, 2017.

Sheff, David, and Nic Sheff. *High.* Boston, MA: Houghton Mifflin Harcourt, 2019.

Sheff, Nic. *Tweak: Growing Up on Methamphetamines.* New York, NY: Atheneum Books for Young Readers, 2018.

Waters, Rosa. *Methamphetamine and Other Amphetamines.* Broomall, PA: Mason Crest, 2015.

American Addiction Centers. "The Effects of Meth on Your Body." DrugAbuse.com, 2019. https://drugabuse.com/featured /the-effects-of-meth-on-your-body.

Blois, Matt. "ERs Emerge as the Frontline in the Meth War." Meth Effect, University of Montana School of Journalism. Retrieved February 8, 2019. http://metheffect.com/MethER-Repercussions .html.

Burch, Kelly. "Meth Hospitalizations More Than Double." The Fix. November 29, 2018. https://www.thefix.com/meth -hospitalizations-more-double.

Drug Enforcement Administration. "Drugs of Abuse: A DEA Resource Guide." US Department of Justice, June 16, 2017. https://www.dea.gov/sites/default/files/sites/getsmartaboutdrugs .com/files/publications/DoA_2017Ed_Updated_6.16.17 .pdf#page=54.

Foundation for a Drug-Free World. "The Deadly Effects of Meth." Retrieved February 8, 2019. https://www.drugfreeworld.org /drugfacts/crystalmeth/the-deadly-effects-of-meth.html.

Foundation for a Drug-Free World. "What Is Meth Made From?" Retrieved February 8, 2019. https://www.drugfreeworld.org /drugfacts/crystalmeth/what-is-meth-made-from.html.

Get Smart About Drugs. "Cassie Haydal, 18, Methamphetamine." DEA, August 17, 2018. https://www.getsmartaboutdrugs.gov /consequences/true-stories/cassie-haydal-18-methamphetamine.

Itzkoff, Dave. "Fathers and Sons, Reliving on Film the Pain of Addiction." *New York Times*, October 12, 2018. https://www .nytimes.com/2018/10/12/movies/beautiful-boy-david-sheff-nic -sheff.html.

McDonnell-Parry, Amelia. "Meth Is Making a Comeback Across

America." *Rolling Stone*, October 8, 2018. https://www
.rollingstone.com/culture/culture-news/meth-comeback-opioid
-epidemic-america-734097.

Morris, Frank. "Methamphetamine Roils Rural Towns Again Across
The U.S." *All Things Considered*, October 25, 2018. https://
www.npr.org/sections/health-shots/2018/10/25/656192849
/methamphetamine-roils-rural-towns-again-across-the-u-s.

National Institute on Drug Abuse. "Drug Facts: What Is
Methamphetamine?" June 2018. https://www.drugabuse.gov
/publications/drugfacts/methamphetamine.

National Institute on Drug Abuse. "What Are the Long-Term Effects
of Methamphetamine Abuse?" September 2013. https://www
.drugabuse.gov/publications/research-reports/methamphetamine
/what-are-long-term-effects-methamphetamine-abuse.

National Institute on Drug Abuse for Teens. "Brain and Addiction."
December 2014. https://teens.drugabuse.gov/drug-facts
/brain-and-addiction.

National Public Radio. "Father and Son Behind 'Beautiful Boy'
Share Their Story of Addiction and Recovery." October 19,
2018. https://www.npr.org/2018/10/19/658781285
/father-and-son-behind-beautiful-boy-share-their-story-of
-addiction-and-recovery.

Partnership for Drug-Free Kids. "Meth Is on the Rise Again: What
Parents Should Know." October 17, 2018. https://drugfree.org
/parent-blog/meth-is-on-the-rise-again-what-parents-should-know.

PBS. "How Meth Destroys the Body." *Frontline*. Retrieved February
8, 2019. https://www.pbs.org/wgbh/pages/frontline/meth/body.

PBS. "What Is Meth?" *Frontline*. Retrieved February 8, 2019.
https://www.pbs.org/wgbh/pages/frontline/meth/faqs.

Recovery Village. "The Dangers of Methamphetamine: Ingredients
and How It's Made." Retrieved February 8, 2019. https://www
.therecoveryvillage.com/meth-addictionmeth-addiction
/dangers-methamphetamine-ingredients-made.

Robles, Frances. "Meth, the Forgotten Killer, Is Back. And It's Everywhere." *New York Times*, February 13, 2018. https://www.nytimes.com/2018/02/13/us/meth-crystal-drug.html.

Schmitt, Olivia. "Addicted to Meth: A Man's Story of Loss and His Journey of Recovery." KWWL.com, November 15, 2018. https://kwwl.com/news/2018/11/15/addicted-to-meth-a-mans-story-of-loss-and-his-journey-of-recovery.

Schuppe, Jon. "Twin Plagues: Meth Rises in Shadow of Opioids." NBC News, July 5, 2017. https://www.nbcnews.com/news/us-news/twin-plagues-meth-rises-shadow-opioids-n776871.

Sekine, Yashimoto, Yasuomi Ouchi, et. al. "Methamphetamine Causes Microglial Activation in the Brain of Human Abusers." *Journal of Neuroscience*. May 28, 2008, 28 (22) 5756–5761.

Sheff, Nic. "My Life as a Teenage Meth Head." The Fix, January 27, 2012. https://www.thefix.com/content/i-was-a-teenage-meth-head-nic-sheff-10010?page=all.

Substance Abuse and Mental Health Services Administration. "Key Substance Use and Mental Health Indicators in the United States: Results from the 2017 National Survey on Drug Use and Health." September 2018. https://store.samhsa.gov/product/Key-Substance-Use-and-Mental-Health-Indicators-in-the-United-States-/sma17-5044.

Suhan, Christine. "Meth Addiction Nearly Took My Life." *Marie Claire*, October 27, 2015. https://www.marieclaire.com/health-fitness/a16607/meth-addiction-nearly-took-my-life.

US Forest Service. "Dangers of Meth Labs." US Department of Agriculture. Retrieved February 89, 2019. https://www.fs.fed.us/lei/dangers-meth-labs.php.

Vergano, Dan. "The Opioid Crisis Is Becoming a Meth and Cocaine Crisis." BuzzFeed News, January 16, 2019. https://www.buzzfeednews.com/article/danvergano/cocaine-meth-overdose-wave.

INDEX

About the Author

Alexis Burling spent many years as an editor and contributor to Scholastic's classroom magazines, including *Storyworks*, *Choices*, and *SuperScience*. She has written numerous books and articles for kids and teens on a variety of topics ranging from current events and career advice to biographies of famous people. Some of her latest books for Rosen Publishing include *Everything You Need to Know About Confronting Violence Against Women* and a biography of power couple Serena Williams and Alexis Ohanian. Burling lives with her husband in Portland, Oregon.

Photo Credits

Cover Daniel Kaesler/EyeEm/Getty Images; p. 5 Shawn Ehlers/WireImage/Getty Images; p. 7 Leszek Czerwonka/Shutterstock.com; pp. 9, 20, 23 © AP Images; p. 13 Hill Street Studios/DigitalVision/Getty Images; p. 15 Comstock Images/Stockbyte/Getty Images; p. 17 © iStockphoto.com/Serghei Turcanu; p. 21 Juanmonino/E+/Getty Images; p. 27 littlenySTOCK/Shutterstock.com; p. 30 fstop123/E+/Getty Images; p. 34 Danai Khampiranon/Shutterstock.com; p. 36 Maskot/Getty Images; back cover and interior speech bubbles sumkinn/Shutterstock.com.

Design and Layout: Nicole Russo-Duca; Editor: Jennifer Landau; Photo Researcher: Sherri Jackson